Harry Hunnybunny's
GRAND PRIZE DAY

WRITTEN BY DOLLY HUNTER

ILLUSTRATED BY DIA KIK

MISSION POINT PRESS

Copyright © 2018 by Dolly Hunter

Illustrations by Dia Kik

All world rights reserved.

No part of this book may be reproduced, stored in a retrieval system, or transmitted in any form or by any means electronic, mechanical, photocopying, recording or otherwise, without the prior consent of the publisher.

Readers are encouraged to go to www.MissionPointPress.com to contact the author or to find information on how to buy this book in bulk at a discounted rate.

Published by Mission Point Press
2554 Chandler Rd.
Traverse City, MI 49686
(231) 421-9513

www.MissionPointPress.com

ISBN: 978-1-943995-88-2
Printed in the United States of America.

"Hurry," cried Mother Hunnybunny, "he'll be here any minute!"

The Mayor of Carrotville was due to arrive any time now. Not only was His Honor coming to HareBurrow, he was coming for a full days visit to the Hunnybunny farm.

Earlier in the week Harry (one of the Hunnybunny children) won a lettuce pie eating contest at the county fair, and the Grand Prize included spending a day with the Mayor of Carrotville.

The Mayor was a truly extraordinary type of fellow. He had been a magician who traveled with the circus before becoming mayor. Knowing this made the Hunnybunny household even more excited.

Mother wanted everything just right for their special guest. But, getting those Hunnybunny children to do their chores was a chore in itself!

"Children, please pick up the yard."

"Please do not nibble on the carrot sticks."

"Please, please, please!"

Finally, it was 2:00 PM and His Honor, the Mayor could be seen coming up the long winding path in his shiny limousine with the official Carrotville flag (a green and orange banner) blowing wildly in the breeze.

"We are very pleased to have you at our farm Your Honor," said Father Hunnybunny.

"I am most happy to be here," replied the Mayor. "Now on with the festivities.

"First I would like to congratulate Harry on his champion pie eating tactics and present him with a blue ribbon."

All the Hunnybunnys clapped and cheered for their brother.

"Wait!" shouted the Mayor. "I also have a very special surprise for Harry.

"As you know, I was a magician years ago and I would like to present Harry with one of my Super Special Cylinders of Beautiful Bubbles. They are magical you know."

Harry and the Hunnybunny family were now jumping with joy.

"Children," called Mother Hunnybunny. "We'll have some lunch now and then we can show His Honor our farm and play some games."

As the lunch was being brought to the picnic table, Harry decided to try his Super Special Cylinder of Beautiful Bubbles.

That they were colors you have never seen, and shapes of circles, hearts, triangles, and stars; any shape or color you could imagine flowed from the Cylinder as he slowly cranked it open.

The Mayor noticed Harry opening the Cylinder and shouted, "Harry! Harry! Wait! I forgot to give you . . ." The Mayor ran toward Harry.

Just then Harry opened the Cylinder a little wider and, with the last crank of the lid, the most wonderful, colorful, large, very very large bubble escaped from the Cylinder, surrounding Harry and the Mayor.

In all his delight, Harry did not notice the gust of wind that came upon them. In one quick moment, Harry and the Mayor had floated into the air.

"Oh, Harry, in all the excitement I forgot to tell you the one rule you must follow when opening the Cylinder. It must be opened after sunset. The colors and shapes are most beautiful, but in sunlight the bubbles become boisterous and this is the result — us up in the air, watching the world go by with no way to land until sunset," exclaimed the Mayor.

"Oh, don't worry Mr. Mayor," Harry said with great excitement, "this is the best prize I have ever won."

A gentle breeze kept them afloat all afternoon. What sights to see! The farm looked like Harry's patchwork quilt Great-Grandma Hunnybunny had made for him, and the trees looked like giant stalks of broccoli.

This ride was all well and good, but Harry was starting to grow tired and he was very hungry. The Mayor reassured Harry as soon as the sun began to set, they would glide back to earth.

In the meantime, the Hunnybunny family wondered if Harry and the Mayor would ever come back.

Sure enough, as the Mayor had promised, they started gliding homeward with the setting of the sun.

"Oh, Harry! Oh, Mayor! We were so worried that you would never return," cried Mother Hunnybunny as she and Daddy and all the children ran towards them.

Harry hugged his mom and dad, and excitedly told them of his magical journey. Then, in a tired Hunnybunny voice, he asked if it was time for lunch yet.

The Mayor and all the Hunnybunnys laughed as they walked back to the house for a very late lunch.

After everyone had eaten, the Mayor announced that it was time for him to leave. "I have had a most delightful day," he said, "and now, before I go, I will show you how the Super Special Cylinder of Beautiful Bubbles works."

As he slowly turned the lid, all of the Hunnybunnys eyes became wide with wonder. Suddenly the most beautiful bubbles appeared in the dark.

The Mayor handed Harry the Cylinder and reminded him again: "Only to open it after dark." Then he waved good-bye as the beautiful bubbles followed him down the path.

The End

Dolly Hunter lives in Traverse City, Michigan, with her husband. This story was written for their young son and daughter in 1986. On and off over the years Dolly tried to find an artist who could draw what she had imagined her story to look like. Although the drawings were very good, they just did not portray the vision in her mind's eye. Ultimately, Harry always found his way back to the drawer.

In 2017, in Grand Rapids, Michigan, Dolly's daughter and son-in-law welcomed Clara into the world. A first grandchild for three very excited sets of grandparents!

Call it what you may — Divine Intervention (of which both Dolly and Dia are very sure), fate or coincidence. Dolly's son-in-law's mother, Dia Kik, started drawing and painting right around the time the story was written. With Clara's birth, Dolly shared her story with Dia and asked if she would be interested in illustrating the story. Dia's sweet and beautiful portrayal of The Hunnybunny's was just what Dolly had envisioned for more than 30 years.

Hence, our adventurous Harry is out of the drawer and here to delight our Sweet Clara, as well as your sweet and oh, so imaginative children!

CPSIA information can be obtained
at www.ICGtesting.com
Printed in the USA
LVHW072356040119
602350LV00003B/23/P